MW01240972

THIS NOTEBOOK
BELONGS TO:

....

....

Made in the USA
Middletown, DE
09 November 2022

14505535R00068